CARD FORTUNE TELLING

Charles Thorpe

foulsham

LONDON · NEW YORK · TORONTO · SYDNEY

foulsham
Yeovil Road, Slough, Berkshire SL1 4JH

ISBN 0-572-01541-0

Copyright © 1989 and 1992 W. Foulsham & Co. Ltd.

Printed in Great Britain by St Edmundsbury Press Ltd,
Bury St Edmunds, Suffolk.

CONTENTS

PREFACE

No one knows the origin of Card Fortune Telling, as it is shrouded in mystery. But right back through the ages, the Hebrews, the Chaldeans, the Egyptians, and the Chinese used cards, or tokens, for this purpose. It is only in modern times that cards have been used for games. In this book some of the older, as well as the newer, systems of fortune telling are described.

It will be seen that in some of the systems there is a fairly close resemblance to astrological lore—some of the cards being used, almost as the planets are, as significators. Then, too, the arrangement is also astrological for some of the layouts.

This book does not propose to justify card fortune telling; it only sets out what are claimed to be the best methods of divining by means of cards. But, on the other hand, it is suggested that a study of the occult will reveal that there may be much more real depth in the subject than appears on the surface.

Acknowledgement is due for some details derived from Sepharial's compendium of *Fortune Telling by Cards—Cartomancy*, to Professor Foli's *Fortune Telling by Cards*, and to *The Tarot*, by Papus.

History teems with instances of successful cartomancy, or card fortune telling. These are well known, and the interest displayed in attempts to foretell the future is felt to be sufficiently great to warrant bringing out a volume of this kind, giving examples of the various arrangements and the rules for reading the cards.

1

INTRODUCTION

As with nearly all subjects of similar character, there is a diversity of opinion as to the real history of the art of divination by cards. Sepharial, for example, inclines to the belief that it is one of the oldest modes of prediction, and that it has been practised in various ways, from the earliest periods. Both the Chinese and the Egyptians, he asserts, had engraved metal plates or tokens, the former of copper and silver, the latter of gold, which they used for the purpose.

The Egyptian plates, 78 in number, were the work of the great magician, Hermes, and contained symbolic matter and numbers, a page on each, of the great Hermetic book. The division of the book was into two arcanas, the major and the minor. The former contained 22 of the plates, the latter the other 56.

It is said by Sepharial that the Hermetic plates contained, in addition to their symbolic figures, astrological material of immense use in divination. 'The 12 signs of the Zodiac, the 7 Sacred Planets, the 36 Decans, the 360 Degrees, and their corresponding genii, of the Zodiac—these symbols entered into the construction of the hieroglyphs.'

Unfortunately, the complete original key to

the mysterious book of Hermes was lost, but some of the lore has been handed down orally, and some partly preserved by secret societies of initiates in all ages. Thus, we have today comparatively modern transcriptions of the more ancient ideas.

Dr Papus, a learned French *litterateur*, has produced the most exhaustive book on the Tarot of the Bohemians. This, he suggests, has been 'transmitted by the Gypsies from generation to generation . . . the primitive book of ancient initiations'. It contains, according to this writer, 'the explanation of the exalted philosophy and science of ancient Egypt'.

Mr A. E. Waite, who wrote a preface to the book throws some doubt on the authenticity of the historical details, but explains the closeness of the parallel between the symbolism of the tarot and the Hebrew Kabbalah, or Hidden Wisdom. This 'work of Papus,' says Mr Waite, 'will appeal only to serious students, and it will be worth their while to take up his elements and seek to construct them independently'.

Another writer on the subject, Professor Foli, tells us that there is no authentic, or verified history of cards going beyond the last five hundred years, though he himself in another place refers to the 'prevalent belief of their antiquity in other forms'.

Ordinary playing cards, as we now know them, seem certainly to have been derived from the Bohemian Tarot; but these in turn seem to have had an origin which is lost in antiquity.

Foli refers to the Gypsy theory. He carries the tradition back beyond Egyptian days to the early Hindus, and to a migration from them of a low caste through Egypt and so to the West.

Recent studies in anthropology, and symbolism generally, certainly afford some grounds for attributing the use of cards or plates of metal to very ancient times. Nearly all our customs have come down to us from very remote periods. In fact, all our laws are really survivals of customs, the first observance of which is beyond all human power to discover.

Professor Foli says, 'It is certain that at first cards were called by the name *naibi*; and the Hebrew and Arabic words *nabi*, *naba*, *nabad*, signify "to foretell". It is also widely believed that the idea of playing games with cards was an afterthought, and that their original purpose was for the practice of divination.'

Coming now to more recent times, we find several names standing out as popular exponents of cartomancy. Madame Lenormand and Etteilla are two of the most famous. Each of these had a special method of laying-out. The significations of the cards themselves are very similar.

Another method is that of Sepharial, whose works on astrology are numerous, profound and dependable. Sepharial bases his methods largely on astrological systems. Then there is the work of Papus, to which we have already referred.

2

THE GENERAL SIGNIFICATION OF THE CARDS

There is a general agreement as to the significations of the individual cards, which are, however, modified by the positions in which they occur in relation to each other. As to the symbolism of the pack as a whole, this is evident when a few correspondences are pointed out. There are four suites—these correspond to the four seasons—spring, summer, autumn, and winter, and to the four divisions of the day—morning, noon, evening, and night. They also correspond to youth, manhood, maturity, and old age.

For determining the general ruling of the cards, diamonds may represent youth; clubs, manhood; hearts, maturity; spades, old age.

In the work of Papus, in dealing with the Tarot cards, the four suites of which are batons, cups, swords, and pentacles, these are shown to correspond with clubs, hearts, spades, and diamonds. Then four general principles are given. The clubs represent enterprise and glory, the hearts love and happiness, spades hatred and misfortune, and diamonds money and interest, or, more briefly, enterprise, love, hatred, and fortune.

In his book, Sepharial details this a little more fully. Diamonds are said to represent life generally, and so are influenced by the other cards. Hearts are generally to denote friendships, sympathy, love attachments, and peace.

Clubs represent power, arising from position, fame, acquirements, or natural accomplishments. Spades, loss and privation—its own meaning is modified if other cards are near to influence the spade. A run of spades by themselves is a very dismal and ominous portent.

When an enquirer desires to consult the cards one of these is alloted to him or her to indicate the enquirer's personality. A man takes a King, a woman a Queen, and the particular suit chosen is governed by the colour characteristics of the consultant.

A very fair man or woman takes the diamond King or Queen as significator. Persons with very light hair, blue or grey eyes, use diamonds. But diamonds are also used to denote those with grey or white hair.

For those of a slightly darker type than the 'diamond people' hearts are used—they are still distinctly of the fair class of complexion, but not so fair as diamond people.

From this it may be inferred that clubs are brown-haired and brown-eyed people. Spades are black-haired folk with very dark eyes, quite black or very nearly approaching it.

A point to which attention must be directed here is that a reversed card has its meaning modified. In some packs it is fairly easy, by noting the difference in the top margins, to detect a reversed card. But generally speaking now that card printing is so regular, it is better to ensure the detection by marking the cards at one end by a pin prick or a little dot.

Generally, the meanings of the cards remain fairly constant for all the methods. Thus a good-omened card is always such—but the particular or specific meaning of it is altered somewhat by the method of using it. For example, the ten of spades by one method means 'losses,' and, if reversed, 'tears'; in another, 'grief,' and, if reversed, 'passing trouble.' The seven of spades may mean 'hope,' and, if reversed, 'friendship'; or it may be 'resolve,' and, if reversed, 'difficulty in love affairs'.

The meanings, or values, of the cards should be well studied and committed to memory, so that when any particular card appears a key to its interpretation is at once presented to the mind of the reader. The word key is used advisedly, because the terms or values are not to be taken as the absolute determination of the cards, but rather as a guide to the specific values in relation.

If there is a run in any particular suit, it will be seen that clubs will be an omen of the very brightest character, while a similar run of spades will indicate the worst possible phases of fortune. A run of hearts will foretell successes in love, of diamonds in money.

Combinations of Court cards are important. Amongst others the following may be noted.

When the Aces come together, they denote new surroundings. How this will affect the future fortune depends upon the influence of the cards that follow them.

Sepharial suggests that the Aces coming together always portend a change of life. Foli thinks they imply danger and financial loss. But this is lessened if they are reversed; three Aces, temporary trouble. Kings coming all together denote business, or, as another authority has it, 'honours, preferment, good appointments': if reversed, of less value, but arriving earlier. Three Kings are a good omen unless reversed; Four Queens imply talk and scandal, or a social gathering spoilt if the cards are reversed. Three Queens denote friendly visits, but, if reversed, possible danger to the consultant. When the Knaves come together, workmen or agents about the house, or roistering and noisy conviviality. Three betoken annoyances from friends. If reversed, the evil is not considerable.

Four tens or four nines stand respectively for good fortune or suprises. Three tens are very bad, but three nines good. Four eights, a mixed omen of success and failure. Three eights, new family ties. Four sevens, trouble is imminent; three, ill-health, loss of friends.

PRELIMINARY RULES AND HINTS

(1) In preparing the pack of cards, the cutting

should never be omitted. It is a necessary part of the proper arranging of the card sequence.

(2) The cutting must be done always by the person seeking the information. It is his or her way of personally influencing the cards.

(3) The cut must be made with the left hand. The reason for this is the same as requires a person to wear the wedding-ring on the left hand. (It follows that a left-handed person must also cut with the left hand. He or she, therefore, should not reverse the process and cut with the right.)

(4) A divination is always worthless if the person seeking the information knows anything about the positions or values of the cards before he or she should. It is fatal to endeavour to cheat.

(5) When a consultation of the cards is repeated, the second and subsequent occasions are meaningless. It is the first time only that can be depended upon.

(6) A divination should never be sought when the answer is already known to the person seeking for the information. The mind then is not free to allow the divination to work uncontrolled.

3

♥ ♣ ♦ ♠

TELLING THE CARDS

FORETELLING BY NINES

This is considered to be the most useful form of card divination in existence. It has been practised for centuries, not only in the UK, but in nearly all the countries of the Continent and in various centres of the Far East. It is true that the method of applying the divination has not always been exactly the same, but it can be affirmed that, in all essential particulars, it has remained unchanged throughout the ages.

The first step is to shuffle the full pack and then to cut with the left hand. Both these actions must be undertaken by the individual seeking to peer into the unknown. That done, the fifty-two cards are laid out in a circle, moving in an anti-clokwise direction. To conserve space it is usual to lap the cards one over the other, so that no more than a third of the width of any one of them is showing.

When the circle is formed, you count from the first card to be laid, and proceeding along in the direction of laying, the 9th, 18th and 27th cards are taken from the formation and they are examined.

These are the messages conveyed by each of the fifty-two cards:

Hearts

Ace—You have a great love for your home and will always strive to make it a place of happiness.

King—You are a person of considerable kindness and are remarkably just and honourable.

Queen—There are signs that you can be fickle when opportunities come your way.

Jack—You are self-centred and think more of yourself than of others who have claims on you.

Ten—Your heart is set on travel and you want to see the world. Things will happen that will allow your wish to be very considerably gratified.

Nine—Yours will be a life in which good luck will play a greater part than ill-luck.

Eight—You have a serious fault in your character. You are well aware of this, yet you spend more effort in trying to hide the defect than would be required to set about eradicating it.

Seven—You will find more happiness in the woods and fields than in streets and buildings. You will, therefore, aim at settling down away from the multitude.

Six—The unmarried who alight on this card are on the verge of 'big things'. The married will experience a considerable measure of

16

'change', all within a short period.

Five—Marriage, in your case, is very much allied to money. Caution should be your watchword, since money often brings misery.

Four—If unmarried, try to forget that there is such a thing as the united state. Let it take its own course naturally. If married, make the most of the moment. Tomorrow belongs to the unknown.

Three—Difficulties will come, but they will not perturb you, since you are level-headed.

Two—Do not pay too much attention to what your relatives advise. Think out your own course and stand squarely on your own feet.

Clubs

Ace—Marriage will bring you more by way of position than of affection.

King—You are a person with brilliant ideas, but you fail to put them into practice.

Queen—You think too much of what others think of you. After all, their opinions do not mean everything.

Jack—You are a 'spectator' rather than a 'performer.' Do not be satisfied to follow the lead of others. Try to set the pace yourself.

Ten—A storm seems to be brewing. Face up to it and note how the black clouds will roll away. Quake in your shoes and the clouds will stay.

Nine—You do not look sufficiently on the

bright side of life. There is much brightness if you will seek it out.

Eight—Are your friends worth all they pretend to be? It is something you may very well ask yourself.

Seven—Count six months from now and wait patiently for what will happen.

Six—Ten more years of hard work and your reward will not fail to attend your efforts.

Five—That temper of yours needs taking in hand. Without it you will be a hundred per cent better individual.

Four—The next three years will see most of your difficulties righted. After that, the passage will be noticeably smoother.

Three—Dark people will cross your path and endeavour to work evil against you. Therefore you should regard all such with a certain degree of caution.

Two—Choose a mascot and wear it, if you are looking for good fortune.

Diamonds

Ace—There is much that will content you awaiting your pleasure. You must make an effort to secure these benefits, however.

King—There is somebody of the opposite sex in whom you repose too much trust.

Queen—You are a person who rules too harshly when you are in a position to command.

Jack—You try your utmost to do unto others

18

as you would they should do unto you.

Ten—Your love for children is your finest quality. It is something of which you have a right to be proud.

Nine—Money is not a substance that will cause you many sleepless nights.

Eight—Your character is composed of many contradictory qualities and you have a very remarkable facility for covering up your defects.

Seven—Your character is easy to read. You are a person who takes the line of least resistance, whether it conducts you to success or in the opposite direction. You should think more before you act.

Six—You are influenced by others far too much. Have a mind of your own.

Five—Vanity is your main defect. Do not think so much of yourself and what others may be thinking of you.

Four—Do not expect too much of your partner in life. Blessed is he or she who expects very little.

Three—You are as sound as a bell and, as a result, people impose on you.

Two—There is a rosy future awaiting you, as long as you make up your mind to deserve it.

Spades

Ace—There is plenty of fun and happiness in store for you, if you will only banish gloomy thoughts.

King—You find enjoyment in doing the next person a good turn, but do not forget that you have a duty to yourself and your own.

Queen—You ought to have more friends among your own sex.

Jack—You have several very keen admirers. It is more than likely that you are so humble that you have overlooked this.

Ten—You will gain much in life and lose much. On the balance you will end up in practically the same state as you began.

Nine—Trifles worry you more than they ought. Look at the big things in life and forget all about the things that hardly matter.

Eight—Wealth and position have too much influence on you. Remember that hapiness can be gained without either.

Seven—Look after the pence and go on looking after them. The pounds do not really matter in your case.

Six—Yours is, or will be, a happy married life, as long as you do not sigh for the moon.

Five—Let things be what they will be, and you will have your full measure of happiness.

Four—'A fool and his money are soon parted' is a maxim you should take to heart. It has for you a special significance.

Three—You like everything of the best and the best is more than you sometimes deserve. Be contended with things more readily and try to see good in everything.

Two—You ponder too much over what could happen, but never does. Forget about the things that do not really exist.

Now that you know the meaning of each card, take the three that have been chosen by the divination and place them in the order they came from the circle; then consider their readings one with another. If a card flatly contradicts one of the others, which must sometimes happen, note that the later card has more force than the earlier one and, therefore, number 2 outweighs to a slight extent the force of number 1.

WHERE TO SEEK HAPPINESS

Take a full pack of cards, shuffle them well and then cut with the left hand. Now deal yourself the five top cards, all face down. Pick out two of these five, putting them on one side. Then spread out the pack on the table in the shape of a fan and, with eyes closed, take two cards at random from the fan. Place these two cards with the three that were retained from the original five. You now have once more five cards.

Take these five cards and examine them, paying particular attention as to which suit is strongest.

A suit is strongest if you have more cards of it than of any other suit. But should there be two cards of a pair of suits, the stronger suit is the one comprising the better cards.

To determine which are the better cards, value them according to the pips and counting a Jack as 11, a Queen as 12 and a King as 13. An Ace, it may be pointed out, has here the value of one. Thus, if you have a ten and a Jack of clubs and a two and a King of spades, and in addition some other card of either hearts or diamonds, the clubs is the strongest suit because it is worth 21 points, while the spades are only worth 15. Naturally, the hearts or diamonds are ruled out because they show fewer cards than the clubs or spades. Now:

(1) When *Hearts* are in the ascendancy, your greatest happiness in life will come from the friendships you will make.

(2) When *Clubs* are in the ascendancy, your greatest happiness in life will be centred on matters connected with business or money matters.

(3) When *Diamonds* are in the ascendancy, your greatest happiness in life will be derived from serving others and tending to their well-being.

(4) When *Spades* are in the ascendancy, your greatest happiness in life will be found in roaming from place to place and gazing at the change of scene. To stay in one spot will prove particularly irksome.

THIS YEAR—NEXT YEAR

Shuffle the full pack of cards and then cut it into two portions, using the left hand for the purpose.

Take the lower portion and deal out the cards

into four heaps, placing the heaps in the positions of the four limbs of a cross—upper, lower, left-hand and right-hand. Be careful to set out the cards in this order, all face down, and only lay one card at a time.

Note particularly that when all the cards of the 'cut' have been laid, there must be *more* than three cards at each point of the cross. Therefore, if the 'cut' is insufficient to provide for this, gather up the cards and go through the entire perfomance again.

Having laid out the cards and seen that there are sufficient to fulfil the above requirement, take the top one from each heap without looking at it and set it aside.

Now turn over what has just become the uppermost card of each heap and place it on its own heap.

The preliminaries being completed, you examine these four face cards and decide where the one of highest value lies. For this, you take no note of the suits but reckon Ace as highest, followed by King, Queen, Jack, ten, and so on down to three and two.

Now:

(1) If the highest card rests on the upper limb of the cross, good fortune will attend you *this year*.

(2) If the highest card rests on the lower limb of the cross, expect good fortune to be yours *next year*.

(3) If the highest card rests on the left-hand limb of the cross, good fortune will come to

you *sometime*.

(4) If the highest card rests on the right-hand limb of the cross, good fortune will await you *never*.

Whenever two cards tie for being the highest, the safest plan is to recommence the whole operation.

THE LUCK OF THE CROSS

The following divination resembles the one just described in many respects, but it is nevertheless different.

After shuffling and cutting with, of course, the left hand, the pack is run through and no cards are turned during the process. While going through the pack, any fifteen cards are thrown out on one side. They may be the first fifteen, the last fifteen or any fifteen, at your own pleasure; but it is imperative that you must not even have a suspicion that you know the value of any card so selected.

Now you take up these fifteen cards, shuffle them and deal them out in the shape of a cross. The first one goes to form the top limb of the cross, the second one the bottom limb, the third one the left-hand limb and the fourth one the right-hand limb. Thereafter, the cards are set out in the same order, but are laid over the cards already in position. The last three cards are set, one after the other, in the central space of the cross.

Thus you have five packets, each consisting

of three cards. It is important to note that the order of laying the cards must be carefully adhered to, and that the whole effect is ruined if any of the cards are known.

You now pick up any one of the four packets. Which you choose is entirely a matter for you to decide; but once you have looked at the three cards of the selected packet, you may not change to some other packet.

On examining the three chosen cards you have the privilege of changing any one, two or three in your hand for a like number in the centre packet, if you so desire. But, of course, the exchange must be done before you know what cards you will receive in return.

Your hand being settled, you take the cards forming the unused part of the pack, and having cut it at random, the uppermost card of the bottom portion is turned.

This card serves as the key card. Look to see if it is odd or even; then examine your hand to see if it adds up to an odd or even amount. In making the addition, all the numeral cards count as their pip values, while Jacks rank as 11, Queens as 12, and Kings as 13.

Finally:

(1) If the key card is odd and your hand totals up to an odd amount, there is good luck awaiting you at no very distant date.

(2) If the key card is even and your hand totals up to an even amount, exactly the same applies.

(3) If the key card indicates one thing and

your hand the opposite, then expect no kindness from the Fates. They are not in a mood to help you.

THREES AND SEVENS

"Will my wish come true?" is something we have all asked ourselves at one time or another. If such a question is exercising your mind at the moment, just consult the Fates through the cards and see what they say.

For this method the most satisfactory arrangement is to get someone to help you with the pack. First, he or she removes all the court cards from the pack and shuffles what remains. Because it is you who are questioning the Fates it is you who must cut the pack, and cutting, as you know, must always be done with the left hand.

Having cut, your helper slowly runs through the pack, dealing one card at a time on to a heap, the backs of all the cards being uppermost.

While your friend is slowly doing this, you choose three cards, one at a time. Note particularly that a card may not be selected once it has been covered by the dealer. In other words you cannot go back.

Take your three cards, faces down, shuffle them up, placing them eventually in line. Read the cards according to their pip values in this way:

Suppose the first is a three, the second an

eight and the third a two, this will give the number 382. Always read tens as noughts, and, of course, there are no court cards to consider as they have all been removed from the pack.

Whatever number your three cards supply, if it is exactly divisible by three or seven, your wish has every prospect of being realised. If it is not divisible by either of these numbers, your hopes are in vain. There is little or no chance of the wish coming true.

It will be recognised that a great deal depends on the order in which the cards are placed. Therefore, it is advisable to place them in line before any are turned over. Then, when their order has been definitely established, each is turned over and replaced in its own position. This prevents the making of any mistakes.

HIGH, MIDDLE AND LOW

Take a pack of cards, shuffle it well, cut with the left hand and reform the pack.

Now deal off the top three cards and look at them. Take the card having the highest value and set it aside. Disregard the two others. Note that the highest card for this purpose is an Ace, whilst two is lowest.

Now deal the next three cards and, on this occasion, set aside the one that has the middle value.

Continue by dealing three more cards and you now set aside the card bearing the lowest value.

Go on in this way by dealing three cards at a time from which you set aside the highest, the middle or the lowest card, as the turn requires.

When the pack is exhausted (there will be a final card over at the end, which is disregarded), you have seventeen cards that have been set aside. Take these seventeen cards and put them into heaps according to the suits.

If *Hearts* are most numerous, you will experience a great deal of happiness in your love affairs.

If *Diamonds*, then a slice of good luck awaits you in affairs of business and money.

If *Spades*, then you must be on your guard when making friendships.

If *Clubs*, then you should avoid the colour green, especially in matters connected with dress.

In every case, should two suits be represented by the same number of cards, the whole performance must be repeated. This holds whether the two suits head the list or not.

Some people perform this particular divination in a slightly different manner. They work through the pack and obtain the seventeen cards, as explained. To these seventeen, they place the final card left over, which was disregarded; then they take the eighteen cards and work through them, finding the high, middle and low, as before. This gives them six cards, which are placed in suits, exactly as was explained in the first method when dealing with the seventeen cards.

THE 'F' CLUE

Not long ago the following was seen at a well-known place in the West End of London.

The pack was shuffled and cut into five portions. A seer did the shuffling, but the cutting was performed, with the left hand, by the person seeking to gain information from the cards.

When these preliminaries had been attended to, the seeker pointed to whichever portion of the pack he or she fancied most, and then the seer picked up the selected portion and ran through the cards, sorting them out as this was done. All the Kings were put together, all the Queens, all the Jacks, and so on, laying them on the table when he had finished.

The seer then explained that each of the thirteen ranks of cards had a particular 'F' meaning attached to it. If one rank of card figured more in the pack selected by the seeker than any other rank, then the seeker could rest assured that the meaning attached to that rank would also describe his or her character very tersely.

Here was the list, with the meanings, used by the seer:

King—Faithful (loyal, trusty)
Queen—Flirt
Jack—Flatterer
Ten—Fastidious (difficult to please)
Nine—Faultless (perfect)

Eight—Fire-brand (one who angers easily)
Seven—Famous (renowned)
Six—Faithless (deceptive, false)
Five—Fearless (bold, intrepid)
Four—Fickle
Three—Facetious (funny)
Two—Frigid (cold, heartless)
Ace—Frivolous (trifler)

Of course, it is quite possible that two ranks of cards might tie for the first place. When this occurs, it is the duty of the seer to mention the fact without stating what the particular ranks happen to be and then the seeker makes another choice from the portions of the pack already set out on the table.

FORTUNE-TELLING WHIST

This form of whist is played in exactly the same way as the usual kind, except that the four players act independently of each other and not as partners, that there are no trumps and that the rank of the cards is slightly different. The Queen is highest, followed by the King, Jack, ten, and so on, down to the Ace, which is lowest.

The game is, first to take as many tricks as possible and second, to win, if possible, a trick in which the Queen and King of hearts figure. From this, it is evident that the person receiving the Queen of hearts in the deal has an excellent chance of winning the most coveted trick of all; but, of course, there is no certainty that he or she will be able to do so. For instance, it is a sheer impossibility when the King and Queen happen to be in the same hand, and it is a lost opportunity also when the King is thrown down by a player coming after the one who holds the Queen.

One point is given to the winner of each trick; but a trick containing both the Queen and King of hearts counts five points. Whoever scores 21 points first is the winner, and to win is to experience some slice of good luck before the appearance of the next full moon.

For many years it has been held that it is unlucky to play this game more than once during the same moon.

THE ZODIAC INDICATOR

As this form of divination makes use of the Signs of the Zodiac, it will be as well to state at the outset the names of the twelve signs and the dates influenced by them. They are:

H—Aries—March 21st to April 20th
C—Taurus—April 21st to May 21st
D—Gemini—May 22nd to June 21st
S—Cancer—June 22nd to July 22nd
H—Leo—July 23rd to August 23rd
C—Virgo—August 24th to September 23rd
D—Libra—September 24th to October 23rd
S—Scorpio—October 24th to November 22nd
H—Sagittarius—November 23rd to December 21st

C—Capricorn—December 22nd to January 20th

D—Aquarius—January 21st to February 19th

S—Pisces—February 20th to March 20th

It will be noted that before each sign a letter is placed. H stands for hearts; C for clubs; D for diamonds; and S for spades.

Now the thing to do is to wish for something. Let it be a reasonable demand that could come true if the Fates were favourably inclined towards you. Therefore, do not wish that a relative will die and leave you a million pounds, nor that in less than twelve months you will be the reigning sovereign of Utopia. Having made your wish, write it down to fix it.

Next, take the pack of cards, shuffle it well and cut with the left hand. Then, with the cards face down, go through the pack, dealing it on to the table. Whenever you feel the impulse, set out a card here and there to represent any one of the Signs of the Zodiac. This is best done by imagining twelve spaces in a vertical row and putting cards in these spaces, as you fancy. Of course, you will follow the order of the Signs, as we give them, but you may put the cards into the spaces in any order you please. When you reach the end of the pack, there should be three cards to represent each Sign. The other cards of the pack are thrown on the table.

Lastly, look at our list and see in which Sign-period your birthday comes. Having found it, note the initial letter placed beside the period concerned. Then turn up the three cards set down by you for this particular period. If the three cards, or two of them, belong to the suit indicated by the initial letter, there is every reason to suppose that the Fates take a kindly view of your wish.

If the cards and the initial letter do not agree, there is still a chance that things will come right for you. This happens when two or three of the cards are of the same colour as the suit indicated by the initial letter.

WHICH IS YOUR LUCKY DAY?

Take a pack and throw out all the cards above the sevens; thus, your short pack will consist of four cards each of the ones, twos, threes, fours, fives, sixes and sevens, i.e., twenty-eight cards in all.

Shuffle them well, cut with the left hand and reform the short pack, preferably with the same hand.

Now set out all the cards in a circle. In order to save space, the usual way of doing this is to lay the cards so that they overlap to the extent of about two-thirds of their width. Be careful, however, to slide the last card under the first, in order that they may all show to approximately the same extent.

Next take a pencil or other pointed article,

hold it in the left hand, close the eyes and revolve the hand seven times, then bring the point down on the circle of cards.

Open the eyes and note the card touched. Proceed from the card signalled out in this way to the first *Ace*, going forward in a clockwise direction. Note which Ace it is. Then go on to the first *two* that comes after the Ace. Again note the suit. Continue until you reach the first *three* and follow in the same manner, until you arrive at the first *four*, *five*, *six* and *seven*. In each case, note the suit, preferably by jotting it down on a slip of paper, thus:

One(Ace)—Clubs

Two—Hearts

Three—Hearts, etc.

Now, without altering the circle in any way, close the eyes and go through the same performance again; but on this occasion, when you open your eyes, travel in an anticlockwise direction and begin by looking for a *seven,* and follow by searching for the *six, five, four,* etc., down to the *one* or Ace.

Having finished this part of the divination, examine your list. If any number has received two red cards in the two trips round the circle, good luck is surely assigned to it. Of course, *one* stands for Sunday, *two* for Monday, and so on up to *seven*, which is Saturday.

Thus, by following these instructions, you can easily find out which day or days in the week, if any, are lucky for you.

THE LUCK OF THE WEEK

This divination deals with much the same objective as that referred to under the previous heading. The method, however, is more or less different. It is one much practised in Eastern countries.

The object is to find out which days of the week are lucky and which unlucky, as far as you are concerned. This, of course, is something which is highly important, as it helps you to decide when to undertake great affairs, and when to lie low.

The first step is to place the nine of hearts on the table, face up. Then the pack is shuffled by you, cut with the left hand and reformed. Next you throw any seven cards out of the pack, choosing them from wherever you like, and these seven cards you arrange around the nine of hearts to form a semi-circle. Naturally, they are placed face down, as you must not know anything about them.

Following all this, you shuffle the pack again, put it as before and reform it. That done, you deal off the seven top cards of the pack and place them, one at a time, on the seven cards forming the semi-circle. This must be done in order, starting from the left.

The last step is to turn over the seven pairs of cards, preserving their order or positions. The first pair, on the left, stands for Sundays, the second pair, Mondays; and so on to the last pair which represents Saturdays. When a pair consists of two red cards, the portent is that the day of the week for which the pair stands will be thoroughly lucky. Two black cards stand for no luck, and where there is a red and a black card there is luck assigned, but it is of no considerable amount. Thus, if the third and fifth pair of cards are red, while the fourth pair is black, you will know that Tuesdays and Thursdays are lucky days for you; but that Wednesdays are just the reverse. You will be very active in your important undertakings on Tuesdays and Thursdays. On Wednesdays, you will avoid all that must be done in your best style.

WHO WISHES TO MEET YOU?

This is a form of divination of interest to the female sex. Two complete packs of cards are taken and each is thoroughly shuffled, separately. They are both cut with the left hand. The first is reformed in the usual way and the top card of the cut of the second pack is set face up.

That done, the first pack is turned, card by card, until the same card is reached as forms the turn-up of the second pack.

Everything now depends on the next few cards. If the card following the pairing card happens to be a King or a Jack, no more cards have to be turned; but if it is neither a King nor a Jack, the next card is turned, and this may go on for five cards, but no more.

If no King nor Jack happens to be found among the first five cards that follow the pairing card, then the answer to 'Who wishes to meet me?' is definitely *nobody*.

If, however, a King or a Jack is found among these first five cards, then the answer to the question is as follows:

King of Hearts—A man of middle age with hair that is neither black nor dark brown.

King of Clubs—A man of forty, at least, with brown hair.

King of Diamonds—A man of middle age with light hair.

King of Spades—A man well past forty, with hair going grey.

Jack of Hearts—A young man with hair that is neither black nor dark brown.

Jack of Clubs—A young man, with brown hair.

Jack of Diamonds—A young man, with light hair.

Jack of Spades—A young man, with dark hair and, most likely, blue eyes.

Note particularly that should there be more than one King or Jack among the five cards, it is only the first one that has any force. The others must be ignored. In fact, you really ought to stop turning the cards immediately one of the eight cards is discovered.

WILL YOUR WISHES BE GRANTED?

The players who desire to find the answer to this important question sit around the table. Then a pack of cards is shuffled and cut by somebody with, of course, the left hand.

Following that, each person writes a reasonable wish on a slip of paper, initialling it. The papers are then collected and put in a box reposing in the centre of the table.

The next step is for the dealer to serve three cards to each player. These are dealt one at a time, in the usual manner.

Now the person sitting on the dealer's left turns his top card and subsequent players follow; but no player may turn a card until the previous person has had time to size up his card and has called 'Ready'.

In this way, the game proceeds until all the cards are turned; then a new deal may be made, if desired. Whenever a new deal is started, the wish box must be emptied and fresh wishes are to be made. Note that no person is permitted to repeat a previous wish; an entirely different one is alone effective.

The greatest boon that can come to a player is to hold the *nine of hearts* because this card has been known for centuries as 'the wish card'. Anyone turning it over is sure to have his or her wish come true.

It is also lucky to turn a card that is one

position higher of the same suit as the card turned by the player immediately before. Thus, if A turns the nine of clubs, it is fortunate for B to turn the ten of clubs, but if C turns the ten of clubs the effect is nothing. B's wish has an excellent chance of coming true.

Note particularly that players must stack their three cards in the order received and they must always play the top card.

It must be understood that the divination is not complete until a person claiming a 'lucky win' has sought out his or her paper from the wish-box and read the wish aloud before the whole company of players.

YOUR FATE

Before attempting this form of card divination, take an Ace, a two, a three and a four from the pack, shuffle them together and draw any one of them at random. Then look at the card and remember that it determines which row in the following 'lay-out' is the one that affects your destiny. Thus, if it is:

(a) The *Ace*, the 1st row is concerned.
(b) The *two*, the 2nd row is concerned.
(c) The *three*, the 3rd row is concerned.
(d) The *four*, the 4th row is concerned.

Having determined this part of the destiny working, return the four cards to the pack which is now thoroughly shuffled; then cut with the left hand and reform the two portions.

Now lay out the first 36 cards of the pack in

four rows, each of nine cards, and be very sure that you commence each row at the right, working towards the left.

There is one card in the 'lay-out' which will tell you something you will be interested to know. It is the last card to be laid of the row decided by the card you drew at the outset.

Pick out this card and note its suit. This is what it tells you:

(a) If belonging to the *first* row and it is:

A Heart—You are likely to rise in the world owing to your own efforts and exertions.

A Diamond—You will have to face difficulties that will cause you many sleepless nights.

A Club—You are about to enter upon a fresh chapter in your life.

A Spade—The coming year calls for cautious action on your part.

(b) If belonging to the *second* row and it is:

A Heart—A specially fortunate period of your life is close at hand.

A Diamond—Do not be over-trusting. There are wolves in sheep's clothing.

A Club—Be firm with those who treat you lightly. Let them understand that you have a will of your own.

A Spade—Have faith in yourself and the troubles that are sure to come will melt away.

(c) If belonging to the *third* row and it is:

A Heart—You will shortly have very good reason for congratulating yourself.

A Diamond—Do not fritter away your opportunities. Grasp them with both hands when they come.

A Club—Riches will never be yours, but you need not worry, since you will always be comfortable.

A Spade—Shake off your doubts and have faith in yourself. All will be well then.

(d) If belonging to the *fourth* row and it is:

A Heart—Pleasures are coming to you from an unexpected quarter.

A Diamond—You are to be rewarded for past deserts.

A Club—Many of your friends will soon envy your good fortune.

A Spade—The Fates are not going to be any too kind to you.

WHAT REVERSED CARDS TELL

Most cards in an ordinary pack appear to be the right way up whether looked at from one edge or from the other. This is the case, for instance, with all the court cards. But if the

Aces are examined, none but the diamond Ace is symmetrical. The others will appear right enough when viewed from one edge, but upside down when glanced at from the opposite edge. Similarly, of hearts, clubs, and spades, the threes, the fives, the sixes, the eights and the nines, and of hearts, clubs, spades and diamonds, the sevens all have a right way and a wrong way up.

This feature of not being symmetrical affected every card in the pack in olden days and the diviners then used the fact for determining their luck.

By a simple process, we can employ the method followed by the ancients and so determine our luck. It is to run through the pack and put a small mark, such as a dot, on the upper left-hand corner of every card. In the case of the non-symmetrical cards, a glance will be all that is needed to see where the dot must go; in the case of the symmetrical cards, we will have to decide ourselves which edge is to be top and which bottom.

When that is done, the pack is shuffled and cut with the left hand, then reformed. After that, each card is dealt on to the table slowly, the reversed cards being put into one heap, the non-reversed cards into another. A reversed card is, of course, one with the mark coming at the lower edge.

These reversed cards are now taken and sorted into four heaps, according to their suits; then they are counted.

If *hearts* are more numerous than the other suits, your share of luck in the immediate future will be very comforting to you.

If *clubs* are more numerous, there is still luck for you in the near future. It will not be so bountiful as in the previous case, but enough to satisfy you, nevertheless.

If *diamonds* head the list, the Fates are passive in your case. There is neither luck nor ill-luck registered against your name.

If *spades* stand first, then the balance of luck is not in your favour.

One thing more. If the total number of cards is odd, the Fates will grant you the favour of a wish. When the cards are odd and spades head the list, let your wish be that each spade be transformed into a heart when the Fates take stock of them. In other cases, wish whatever is dearest to you, as long as it is reasonable.

It was always held to be unlucky to test this form of divination on Fridays or twice during the same moon.

THE FOUR ACES

Take the four Aces from a pack and set them in line, faces up, on the table. Note that the—

Heart stands for love affairs.

Club stands for business matters.

Diamond stands for home affairs.

Spade stands for social affairs.

Next shuffle the remainder of the pack and cut it with the left hand. Then write on a slip of paper any eight numbers ranging between 1 and 48, the first and last numbers inclusive.

Following this, deal out the cards singly on to the table, counting them as you go. When you reach any card with a number corresponding to a number set out on the list, place it on one side. By the time you have run through the pack, you will have put aside eight cards. It must be understood that the pack and all the cards are handled with their faces down, the Aces excepted.

Take the eight cards and set two on each Ace. This can be done in any way that is desired. The only rules are that two cards must cover each Ace and you must not have the slightest notion what they are.

Now turn to the Ace of hearts and the two cards covering it. If both the covering cards are hearts, you are sure to be very lucky in your love affairs. If only one of the cards is a heart you will be just lucky. If neither is a heart, the chances are that you will be neither lucky nor unlucky. Thus, there is nothing in this particular divination which definitely points to ill-luck.

As with hearts, so with the other suits. Thus the complete reading may be set out as follows:

On the Ace of Hearts:
(a) Two heart cards—Very lucky in love affairs.

(b) One heart card—Lucky in love affairs.

(c) No heart cards—Neither one nor the other is indicated.

On the Ace of Clubs:

(a) Two club cards—Very lucky in business affairs.

(b) One club card—Lucky in business affairs.

(c) No club cards—Neither one nor the other is indicated.

On the Ace of Diamonds:

(a) Two diamond cards—Very happy in home affairs.

(b) One diamond card—Happy in home affairs.

(c) No diamond cards—Neither one nor the other is indicated.

On the Ace of Spades:

(a) Two spade cards—Very happy in social life.

(b) One spade card—Happy in social life.

(c) No spade cards—Neither one nor the other is indicated.

THREES

Take a full pack, shuffle it well, cut with the left hand and reform the pack with the same hand. Then deal out the cards, throwing every third card into a separate heap. This latter heap will consist of 17 cards by the time the pack is exhausted.

The second step is to take the 17 cards, to shuffle and cut them exactly as before, and then to deal them out, throwing away every third card into a separate heap. This heap will eventually contain five cards.

The third step is to shuffle and cut the five cards as was done twice previously, and then the middle card of this short pack is taken out and turned face uppermost.

Step four is to take another pack, to shuffle it and then to cut it with the left hand. Having cut, the top card of the lower portion is turned face uppermost.

If this turned card belongs to the same suit as the card which was turned previously, any wish that you may have already written on a piece of paper will come true. When the card that was singled out of the pack, by resolving the deals into 'threes', happens to be the *nine of hearts*, your wish will be granted whether the 'turn-up' is a heart or not.

COMBINED CARDS

Here is an easy way of extracting from the cards some information that should prove useful to you.

First shuffle the pack, cut it with the left hand and reform it with the same hand. Still using only the left hand, push the pack so that the cards are splayed out in the form of a horseshoe, on the table. In doing this, it is preferable to allow the third finger to force the cards into the required shape. The third finger, it may perhaps be useful to add, is the one next to the little finger.

The horseshoe being formed, you now choose any two cards you like, and, naturally, you do not know what they are, since they are all lying with the backs up.

When the two cards have been chosen, you look at them and note the suits. The two cards can belong to the same suit or to two different suits. According to what they happen to be so your future is foretold.

When your cards are:

(a) *Two Hearts*, there is much domestic happiness in store for you. Love will play a large part in your life and friendships will add greatly to your joys.

(b) *Two Clubs*, you will experience a future that will show a gradual rise in your status. Your advice will be sought by many and you will not want for money.

(c) *Two Diamonds*, they show that you are an up-to-date person who is anxious to try the new innovations of life. You will remain young in mind to the last; but there is a clear portent that your seeking after all that is new will not always lead you to happiness.

(d) *Two Spades*, there are signs that misfortune will come your way. Life will not always be rosy.

(e) *One Heart and One Diamond*, you will have successes through your own exertions.

(f) *One Heart and One Club*, you are marked out for the role of peacemaker.

(g) *One Heart and One Spade*, there is a danger that you may be drawn into unfortunate love tangles.

(h) *One Club and One Diamond*, you will be fortunate in how you handle your money. Business, as far as you are concerned, will thrive.

(i) *One Diamond and One Spade*, you should avoid unnecessary risks.

(j) *One Club and One Spade*, there is evidence that you will grow into the habit of being despondent over unnecessary things if you do not check yourself.

THE LOVER'S TRIANGLE

Take a pack of cards, shuffle it well, cut with the left hand, reform the pack; then set out the cards on the table in the following way:

(1) Taking the cards in the order they come from the pack, set out a horizontal row of nine of them, beginning at the right and working to the left.

(2) Below the first row, set out a second horizontal row, consisting of eight cards. Leave the space blank under the first card of the top

row. Thus, the first card of the second row comes under the second card of the first row.

These two rows will, therefore, be arranged thus:

```
9   8   7   6   5   4   3   2   1
8   7   6   5   4   3   2   1
```

(3) Now deal out a horizontal row of seven cards. Place No. 1 of this row under No. 2 of the previous row.

(4) Follow with a row of six cards, placing No. 1 of this row under No. 2 of the previous row.

(5) Follow with further rows of five, four, three, two and one cards, preserving the indented order in each instance and always dealing from right to left. All cards are set face up.

Your completed tableau now presents the following appearance:

```
9   8   7   6   5   4   3   2   1
8   7   6   5   4   3   2   1
7   6   5   4   3   2   1
6   5   4   3   2   1
5   4   3   2   1
4   3   2   1
3   2   1
2   1
1
```

This is known as 'The Lover's Triangle'. When it has been set out, there are seven cards left over. Place these, face up, in a position away from the triangle.

Now to discover what the formation reveals.

(1) If No. 9 in the top row is a heart, the consultant's love affairs will be fortunate; they will be especially so when there are more hearts among the seven 'left over' than there are cards of the other three suits.

(2) In the case of a single woman, if the *Queen of Hearts* figures in the horizontal or vertical rows composed of the cards 9, 8, 7, 6, 5, 4, 3, 2, 1, then marriage will take place in the near future.

(3) If the *Queen of Hearts* figures in the horizontal or vertical rows composed of the cards 7, 6, 5, 4, 3, 2, 1, then marriage will be some little time ahead, probably within the next few years.

(4) If the *Queen of Hearts* figures in the horizontal or vertical rows composed of the cards 5, 4, 3, 2, 1, then marriage is a long way ahead. It will not be soon.

(5) In the case of men lovers, the readings of (2), (3), and (4) above, are exactly the same, except that the key card is the King and not the Queen of hearts.

THE STAR OF FORTUNE

This is a very old form of divination and though it requires rather more by way of preliminary arrangement than many of the other layouts in this book, it is well worth the trouble.

First of all, the querent has to be matched. The querent is, of course, the person whose fortune is being revealed, and the matching is done as follows:

A lady with light hair and colouring is matched with the Queen of hearts.

A lady with brown hair and colouring is matched with the Queen of clubs.

A lady with reddish hair and colouring is matched with the Queen of diamonds.

A lady with black hair and dark colouring is matched with the Queen of spades.

Similarly:

A man with light hair and colouring is matched with the King of hearts.

A man with brown hair and colouring is matched with the King of clubs.

A man with reddish hair and colouring is matched with the King of diamonds.

A man with black hair and dark colouring is matched with the King of spades.

Those with grey or white hair are not catered for in this divination as the reading is essentially for young people who have not yet developed their full characters.

Having determined the matching card of the consultant, the card in question is taken from the pack and laid face up on the table, where it serves as the centre of the star that is about to be formed.

The remaining 51 cards are then shuffled, cut with the querent's left hand, and the pack re-formed.

The querent takes the pack at this point, and slowly deals out the cards, all face up, placing them in the following positions:

    1st—Above the matching card.

    2nd—Below the matching card.

    3rd—At right side of the matching card.

    4th—At left side of the matching card.

    5th—Above the 1st card.

    6th—Below the 2nd card.

    7th—Beside the 3rd card.

    8th—Beside the 4th card.

This setting should now form a cross, arranged as follows:

```
        5
        1
   8 4 M 3 7
        2
        6
```

Then, proceeding with four more cards, the positions assigned to them are:

    9th—In the space between 5 and 7.

    10th—In the space between 6 and 8.

    11th—In the space between 5 and 8.

    12th—In the space between 6 and 7.

The *Star of Fortune* is now complete and is read in the following manner:

    1st—If more than four cards forming the star belong to the same suit as the matching card, then the querent may be happy in the knowledge that his or her future will be one of success and prosperity. When this is the case, there is no need to proceed further with the reading. The star has divulged sufficient to please the querent.

2nd—But if the suit of the matching card does not predominate in the lay-out there are still hopes for success and good fortune. Thus, if the nine of the matching suit forms one of the cards in the star, the consultant has only to wish for these favours and they will materialise. He or she may wish for any one reasonable thing and it will be granted.

3rd—If neither the 1st nor the 2nd opportunities occur, then the consultant should examine the four 'flying' cards. These are numbered 9, 10, 11 and 12.

If 9 is the same colour as 5 and 7;

If 10 is the same colour as 6 and 8;

If 11 is the same colour as 5 and 8;

If 12 is the same colour as 6 and 7;

If any one of these four conditions exist, then there is plenty of good fortune and success awaiting the querent. Should the whole four exist, his or her fortune would be marvellously attractive.

4th—Lastly, if the inner ring or the outer ring around the matching card be composed of cards of the same colour, then the querent has again every reason to be pleased and satisfied. This means that if the cards numbered 1, 2, 3 and 4, or 5, 6, 7 and 8 are either all red or all black, good fortune is predicted.

TO BE OR NOT TO BE

Everybody has a preference for one suit over another. This is readily noticed if we listen to a roomful of people playing such games as whist or bridge. My preference is for hearts, but that is merely by the way.

What I want you to do is to take the complete suit, which has earned your preference, from the pack, shuffle the 13 cards thoroughly, and then to place them in a line, faces down, on the table.

That done, you take the complementary suit to the one that has been singled out for your preference, thus:

When your preference is—

Hearts, the complementary suit is Clubs.

Diamonds, the complementary suit is Spades.

Clubs, the complementary suit is Hearts.

Spades, the complementary suit is Diamonds.

This complementary suit is shuffled and placed in a line below the previous line, in such a way that one card is exactly under one card, all along the line.

Having completed these arrangements, the 26 cards are turned, but their original positions must be preserved.

You now have thirteen pairs of cards, a pair consisting of one card in the top row and the card immediately below it in the bottom row.

Look at each pair in turn and note whether the higher-valued card is in the top or bottom row. For purposes of valuation, reckon the order of rank as Ace highest, two lowest, and the other cards in their usual sequence.

If the upper row, which is the one standing for your preference, consists of more 'higher-valued' cards than the row below, then whatever you wish *will be*. If the opposite is the case, then your wish *will not be*.

As an illustration, suppose the two rows happen to fall thus:

J, 9, 6, A, K, 5, 3, 10, 4, 8, 7, Q, 2
5, K, 4, 7, Q, J, 2, 9, 3, 8, 6, 10, A.

The upper row beats the lower row in the 1st, 3rd, 4th, 5th, 7th, 8th, 9th, 11th and 12th positions. It ties at the 10th and loses at the others. Therefore in an example such as this, your wish would come true.

THE HORSESHOE

This particular divination has a special application, for it tells unmarried members of the female sex facts about marriage, in so far as it affects them.

This is how it works: An unmarried woman takes the pack, shuffles it, cuts it with the left hand and reforms the pack. Next, she deals the first six cards from the top of the pack into a heap, and places the heap aside, as it has no further use.

Following that, she deals the seventh card to a fresh heap. The next two cards are thrown aside, but the third card is placed on the new heap. Thereafter every third card is added to this heap, until the heap consists of seven cards.

The seven cards are now taken and, with their backs up, they are shuffled about on the table so that there is no possibility of any of them being known.

The unmarried woman now picks up the seven cards with her right hand and places them on the table, with her left hand, in the form of a horseshoe, the horns or points of which must be turned away from her.

Everything is now ready. With her left hand she turns over the left-hand card of the formation and thereafter she turns all the cards in their order, using her two hands alternately.

The cards being visible now, she examines them. If by a lucky chance, the two horns of the shoe happen to be formed by two Aces, she will marry at an early date and it will be a prosperous marriage.

This, however, is a very unusual formation of the cards which occurs perhaps only once in a thousand times. When the horns are not formed by two Aces, she totals up the value of the seven cards, reckoning all court cards as tens and all numeral cards according to their pip values.

If the total comes to an odd number, marriage will take place. It will be soon if there are more *heart* cards than any other suit. It will not be quite so soon when there are more *club* cards than any other. It will be a fair time hence when *diamonds* are most numerous, and it will be in the dim future when *spades* is the leading suit.

When the total value of the cards is even, the fates seem to suggest that marriage is doubtful.

This is a very old form of divination and there was an idea amongst those who practised it that its portents were only reliable on the first occasion that an unmarried woman attempted it.

SPRING, SUMMER, AUTUMN AND WINTER

The following is a game played by gipsies while sitting round the camp fire. It is really for young people.

From an ordinary pack, the twelve court cards are taken and well shuffled. Note that Aces are not court cards.

A member of the company then takes the short pack and presents it to the person sitting on his or her left. This individual cuts the pack, using the left hand for the purpose. The first person now turns the top card of the cut. This card provides a divination respecting whoever cut the pack.

The divination is found by consulting the list below, but it is first necessary to ask the person concerned when he or she was born, because the birth time affects the reading. There are four different tables, one for those born in spring (March to May), another for those born in summer (June to August), a third for those born in autumn (September to November) and a fourth for those born in winter (December to February).

Here are the readings:

When the consultant was born in spring

King of Hearts—Being of a kindly nature, people like you, and many will hope to be your partner in life.

Queen of Hearts—You will have many chances of being happily married, but as you are fickle you will spoil some of them.

Jack of Hearts—You will spoil your chances of marriage through a somewhat exalted opinion of yourself.

King of Clubs—You have a great deal of common sense and are not likely to throw away your chances of marriage.

Queen of Clubs—Do not worry about what others say and think. If you like him (or her), go ahead and make two people happy.

Jack of Clubs—You are likely to let a rival step in and carry off the person you love.

King of Diamonds—You are too trusting with members of the opposite sex.

Queen of Diamonds—You might very easily spoil your chances by being too over-bearing.

Jack of Diamonds—Love will not be all a bed of roses, but kindness will overcome most of the difficulties.

King of Spades—Do not think that love requires you to be a doormat. Have a will of your own.

Queen of Spades—While seeking your life partner, do not neglect your friends.

Jack of Spades—Do not be so humble. There are several people who have a very affectionate regard for you.

When the consultant was born in summer

King of Hearts—You are too generous and will cause yourself some unhappiness in love affairs, because you are afraid to hurt people's feelings.

Queen of Hearts—You are not certain of your own mind; consequently you will fail to say 'yes,' when it will be best for you to say it.

Jack of Hearts—Love will give you many unhappy moments, because you have curious notions as to how 'he' or 'she' should be treated.

King of Clubs—You will have many chances of marrying well, and you will seize the best of them.

Queen of Clubs—You suffer from an inferiority complex, which may very likely stand in the way of happiness.

Jack of Clubs—You will fall in love with someone who will not return your affection.

King of Diamonds—Be firm but not unkind to the one who has received your affections. A soft nature will not lead to happiness.

Queen of Diamonds—Treat him (or her) exactly as you would like to be treated. It is the only way in your case.

Jack of Diamonds—You will have to exercise a good deal of patience, if your married life is to bring all the happiness you want.

King of Spades—Play the part of lover, even though the wedding-day has long since passed away.

Queen of Spades—Your life-partner will not be found where you think.

Jack of Spades—There is a very pleasant surprise for you. It will happen after the engagement.

When the consultant was born in autumn

King of Hearts—Let your courting days be as happy as they may. Your happiest time will be after the wedding ceremony.

Queen of Hearts—You ought to marry a strong-willed person, since you need guidance.

Jack of Hearts—Do not have two strings to your bow. If you do, there is a world of trouble ahead.

King of Clubs—Yours will be a very happy married life.

Queen of Clubs—Do not be half-hearted in your affections once you have made up your mind.

Jack of Clubs—Do not select riches when you want affection. The person who marries money works for a low wage.

King of Diamonds—Take your partner into your confidence and let him (or her) share all your joys and all your sorrows. There is trouble ahead if you do otherwise.

Queen of Diamonds—Do not be in a hurry to take the first person who returns your affections. You are too easily impressed by faces.

Jack of Diamonds—Your love affairs will not run smoothly until after you are married.

King of Spades—Do not allow yourself to take your lover for granted. You may have arranged everything, but even then a calamity may happen if you do not keep your affections in the forefront.

Queen of Spades—There is a mystery about your love affairs. What is it?

Jack of Spades—Your courting days will not provide the happiest period of your life. That will come after.

When the consultant was born in winter

King of Hearts—You are not likely to make any mistakes as to where it will be wise to place your affections.

Queen of Hearts—Stick to the one you love and there is abundant happiness awaiting you.

Jack of Hearts—Do not hope for a happy married life unless you are prepared to take the rough with the smooth.

King of Clubs—You will need to be an optimist if your love affairs are to prove a success.

Queen of Clubs—Make quite sure of what you expect from love before it is too late.

Jack of Clubs—A pretty face or a handsome one is not everything. Do not judge too much by appearances.

King of Diamonds—Do not let your affections be swayed by money or position. They really count very little.

Queen of Diamonds—Do not let outsiders come between you and your lover.

Jack of Diamonds—Do not be in a hurry to make up your mind. The first to come into your life will not be the best.

King of Spades—You will be fortunate in your final choice.

Queen of Spades—By playing your cards sensibly you can have almost everything you long for.

Jack of Spades—There is ample evidence that your married life will be crowned with happiness.

In conclusion, it should be added that when one person playing this camp-fire game has had his (or her) reading revealed, the others taking part have theirs read in turn. The person whose love-fortune has just been told takes the pack and shuffles it. The neighbour on the left cuts and the reading always affects the one who cuts.

62

WISHES AND WISHING

As is well known, the nine of hearts is called 'the wish card,' since it has long been reckoned to have peculiar properties where wishes are concerned. There are several games which make special use of this card, and the following may be recommended.

The players sit round a table and each writes his or her wish on a scrap of paper.

The papers are then collected and put aside for the time being.

The next thing is to procure a pack of cards and to remove the nine of spades from it. Then the 51 cards that are left are dealt round to the players. It usually occurs that some people will be given one card more than others; but no notice is taken of this.

Play follows on the lines of the popular game 'Old Maids', though there are certain differences. The players look at their cards and throw out of their hands any pairs they happen to hold. A pair is, of course, any two cards of the same rank but of different suits. Here it must be mentioned that the nine of clubs pairs with the nine of diamonds and that the nine of hearts pairs with nothing. Therefore, if a hand contains the nine of hearts and another nine, either of clubs or diamonds, no pairing may be done with them.

When all the preliminary pairing is done, the players hold their cards in a fan, backs towards the other players, and each person takes it in turn to select a card at random from the neighbour on the right. It is cheating to hold a pair and not throw it out.

As play proceeds, pairs are made and thrown out, with the consequence that the hands grow smaller and smaller, until at last one person holds nothing but the nine of hearts. That person is the winner: Fate has singled him out to have his, or her, wish realised in the near future. But fate is not fully satisfied until this lucky individual reads aloud the wish which he or she previously wrote on paper.

If the winner of a game decides to take a hand in a further game, an entirely fresh wish is required.

YOUR LUCKY NUMBER

In certain of the remote parts of America, where people pin their faith to signs and portents, a person often carries out the following practice when he (or she) wants to find out what number will guide his fortunes.

He takes a pack of cards and gathers from it all the numeral cards from one to nine, both inclusive. This gives 36 cards. These are shuffled thoroughly; then he cuts the pack 36, 72 or 99 times without altering the sequence of the cards in the pack. Each time he cuts he notes down on a piece of paper the number of the card that appears.

When the full number of cuts has been satisfied, he consults the list to see which card has
come up most. The number of this card he then
takes as being the number which is likely to
bring him luck.

THE GIPSY'S METHOD

Though many people regard gypsies with
often unfounded prejudices, it is universally
agreed that in some mysterious manner they
have curious powers of seeing into the unknown and that, when they predict a person's
future, what they say is generally right in substance.

All that being so, it is interesting to be able to
set out here how a gipsy will answer the question 'Shall I marry?' using playing cards for
providing the reply.

Let us imagine that you put this question to
one of these interesting women. She will pro-
duce a pack of cards—usually very much
used—and take out the suit of hearts. These
thirteen cards she will shuffle and then ask you
to cut with the left hand. Probably she will
exhort you to think deeply about the wish as
you do the cutting.

The top card of the cut is then turned and
according to what it happens to be so she will
delineate the answer. Here are the answers that
affect the whole suit of thirteen cards:

Ace—Yes, and you will have a happy family.

King—It is uncertain because dark clouds

appear upon the scene. Make your request again in a few months' time and the clouds may have passed away by then.

Queen—Everything will be arranged, but it may not happen.

Jack—Look around; your partner is waiting for you.

Ten—It is unlikely, because when you have the opportunity you will expect perfection and it will not be forthcoming.

Nine—There are many chances for you and you will be slow in taking them.

Eight—Yes, you will marry and, later on, you may wonder why you took the step.

Seven—Everything is being prepared for the great event.

Six—You will marry and you have the chance of making or marring your wedded life. Happiness will depend more on you than on your partner.

Five—You will marry and be happy.

Four—It hardly seems possible that you will be satisfied with whatever happens.

Three—Yes, you will marry, but do not jump at the first opportunity presenting itself.

Two—You will have one chance. It will be worth taking.

LUCKY DAY FOR MARRIAGE

In England it was the custom some two to three centuries ago for a girl to decide upon her wedding-day by the help of a pack of cards.

We will describe how she used the cards as 'Miss Modern' may feel disposed to follow the practice.

The pack was taken, well shuffled and cut with the left hand. The pack being reformed, the girl dealt off the cards one by one, taking from the deal the seventh, ninth and twelfth cards.

Then an almanac was consulted to see when the seventh, ninth and twelfth day following the new moon came. These three days were considered to be the only lucky ones in each lunar month for the ceremony. The cards were used to decide which of the three days was the most propitious.

Turning the three cards, their suits were noted. Hearts was taken to be the most satis-factory, followed by clubs, diamonds and spades, in that order.

Thus, if on turning the cards the ninth one happened to be a heart while the other cards belonged to the remaining suits, it was clear that when the marriage was celebrated on the ninth day of the moon, it would turn out most fortunately.

If hearts did not figure among the three cards, but there was a club standing for the twelfth day, then that was the best day during the lunar month for the ceremony.

Should there be two cards belonging to the leading suit, the one of higher rank indicated the propitious day.

From all this, it will be recognised that it was very necessary to remember which card was which on dealing out the seventh, ninth and twelfth from the pack.

4

♥ ♣ ♦ ♠

THE PIQUET PACK OF CARDS

The following methods of divination to be described are based on the Piquet pack of 32 cards, which finds favour on the Continent. The 32 cards are taken from the ordinary playing pack of cards, you simply discard all the lower value cards, from two to six, both inclusive. The cards, therefore, run from the seven to the Ace. The meanings of the cards are given here in full. The Kings, Queens, and Jacks represent people and thoughts.

Sometimes it is necessary before conducting a reading to remove a card from the pack to represent the enquirer. This is usually a King or Queen, depending on the sex of the enquirer: hearts representing blonde types; diamonds representing fair people; clubs representing brunettes; and spades representing very dark people. If preferred, the pack can be cut and the exposed card would indicate the suit to be used.

The Club Suit

Ace—Money, good news, happiness. If reversed, it is of short duration.

Ten—Fortune, social success, luxury. If reversed, a sea voyage.

Nine—Unexpected gain. If reversed, a trifling present.

Eight—A dark person's affections. If reversed, unhappiness will result from it.

Seven—A small sum of money. If reversed, money troubles.

The Heart Suit

Ace—A letter, pleasant news. If reversed, a visit from a friend.

Ten—Happiness and success. If reversed, a disappointment.

Nine—This is the wish card, and if it turns up near the enquirer's own Court card, the wish will be granted. If reversed, some passing anxiety in connection with the wish.

Eight—A fair person's affections. If reversed, indifference in place of love.

Seven—Pleasant thoughts, tranquillity, If reversed, weariness.

The Diamond Suit

Ace—A letter, If reversed, bad news.

Ten—Journey or change of abode. If reversed, it will not be fortunate.

Nine—Annoyance, delay. If reversed, a quarrel.

Eight—Love making. If reversed, unsuccessful.

Seven—Mockery, unpleasant news. If reversed, scandal.

The Spade Suit

Ace—Pleasure of an emotional nature. If reversed, grief, news of a death.

Ten—Tears, sometimes a prison. If reversed, a brief affliction.

Nine—Tidings of a death or failure. If reversed, loss of a near relation.

Eight—Warning of illness. If reversed, a marriage broken off.

Seven—Slight annoyances. If reversed, folly on the enquirer's part.

Speaking generally, the Heart cards govern the affairs of the home, and therefore the love affairs of the enquirer. Diamonds govern financial and business matters; Clubs are the lucky cards; while Spades are the evil ones, governing ill-health, death, financial loss and ruin. They also represent illicit love affairs.

These general meanings should be borne in mind when looking at the type card that represents the enquirer—one suit or the other is sure to be in ascendancy near the type card.

If a number of Court cards run together, it is a sign of much social hospitality or visiting: gaiety of all kinds. Two red tens coming together foretell a wedding; two red eights new clothes. A Court card coming between two cards of similar denomination (such as two tens, two sevens, etc.) shows that the person represented by the Court card will be involved in legal trouble.

The cards should be cut with the left hand for divination purposes, and a round table is always preferred; it is generally believed that the cards do not 'tell' so truly when the enquirer spreads them on his or her own account—in such a case, it is usual to ask some friend to act as intermediary and make the enquiries on your behalf.

71

PAST, PRESENT, AND FUTURE

The pack of thirty-two cards must be well shuffled by the enquirer and cut with the left hand into two heaps, which can be as equal or unequal in size as the enquirer fancies.

After the cut, the two heaps must not be placed together again until the top card of each has been laid aside, face downwards, to form special 'Surprise' cards, to be examined later. The remaining cards are then squared up and dealt into three heaps of ten cards, which represent respectively the Past (left-hand heap), the Present (centre), and the Future (right-hand heap).

The ten cards of the first heap, the Past, should be spread in a row from left to right and then examined for pairs, triplets, and quadruplets, according to our Table of Meanings. You should carefully note all reversed cards as they tend to lessen the good predicted, or increase the evil, as the case may be. Such cards usually refer to opportunities lost. It is also helpful to notice which suit predominates in each heap, clubs being the most fortunate and spades the most unfortunate. This predominance of colour shows whether the greater amount of success has been reached by the enquirer or is still to come.

After this the cards should be read singly, interpreting their individual meanings, from right to left of the row.

Next, the centre heap, representing the Present, is similarly examined and then the Future.

Finally, the Surprise is consulted to see what unexpected event is going to influence the life and fortunes of the enquirer.

THE FOUR ACES

This is a simple method for determining a single question or wish. The thirty-two cards are shuffled by the enquirer—the diviner then deals off thirteen cards, face upwards on to the table and makes a careful search for the four Aces. If any are found, place them, face up, by themselves. The remainder of the pack, including what are left of the thirteen, are then re-shuffled as before, and the diviner again deals out thirteen cards and searches for further Aces.

This can be done for a third time, but that is all. The earlier the four Aces appear, the better it will be for the enquirer—if in the first deal, it is exceptionally fortunate; if in the second, it is certainly good luck—as a rule, they are not completed until the third attempt has been made.

Those that appear in each deal should be kept separate, as it is important to notice the order in which the suits appear. This will clearly show the amount of effort needed before the wish or question is satisfactorily answered—for instance, if the spade Ace appears first of all, the enquirer must be prepared to face trouble and difficulty, even if all four Aces appear in the course of the first deal.

This is a useful method to know, as several questions can be dealt with in a short time, and there is no need to remember any list of meanings. It is as well to limit the questions to three, however, as the cards are never so reliable when overworked, or tired.

Another simple method for answering a single question is worked with the full pack of fifty-two cards. First remove the type card representing the enquirer, King or Queen, as it happens to be. Then have the fifty-one cards well shuffled and cut into three heaps of any size. They should be cut towards the right by the left hand—the enquirer makes the first cut, placing the upper portion of the pack on the right and then cuts this latter heap into two.

The diviner takes the centre heap (originally the middle of the pack) face down in his or her hand, adds to it the right-hand heap (originally the top of the pack) and finally the left-hand heap goes on top. Now make a circle of forty-two cards, face down, on the table—inside this make a triangle of the remaining nine cards.

The enquirer must now turn over any fifteen cards, replacing them, face upwards, in the original positions. When this is done, read them according to the number of each suit exposed.

THE SEVEN ANSWERS

The thirty-two cards should be shuffled and cut once, as usual with the left hand, and the enquirer should wish once during this process.

Then the cards are dealt out, one by one, so as to form seven piles—six of these to form a semi-circle—the cards being placed face downwards while the seventh heap is built in the centre and the cards are dealt face upwards.

The seven packs represent 'yourself' (i.e., the enquirer); 'your home'; 'what you expect'; 'what you don't expect'; 'the Surprise'; 'what is sure to come true'; and 'your wish'.

It will at once be noticed that some heaps will contain five cards each, others only four each. The heaps should be arranged from left to right—the first card dealt starting the heap on the extreme left and the seventh card going face upwards, in the centre.

Some diviners employ this method but only use seventeen cards—the pack is shuffled and cut as before, but only the first seventeen cards are dealt. This method is certainly simpler, as the heaps only contain two or three cards each; it is also thought to be a great advantage, as the exposed cards naturally vary greatly as regards the proportion from each suit. If you use the full pack, there must of necessity be eight of each suit; whereas if only seventeen are dealt, six or seven or even eight of one suit might appear on the table, and it is obvious that the preponderance of any suit would greatly affect the reading.

Some diviners object to the seven packs, maintaining that it is false art to have one heap for 'what you don't expect,' and another for 'the Surprise'. The sixth heap is also rather feeble, and certainly looks as if it had originally been included to make the number uneven. This School of Diviners therefore deal off thirteen cards only from the full pack of thirty-two, and build up only five heaps for 'yourself'; 'your home'; 'what you expect'; 'the Surprise'; and 'your wish'.

A WEEK'S HAPPENINGS

The enquirer should shuffle the pack and cut the cards with the left hand into three heaps, as before.

The diviner now takes the top card of each heap face downwards and places them so as to start a row of fifteen cards, the top card of the left-hand heap being first removed. The cards are then re-shuffled and cut as before, the diviner again removing the top card from each heap and adding them to the row. This is repeated five times, so that fifteen cards, face downwards, are ranged on the table from left to right.

The diviner now turns over, face upwards, the extreme card at either end and reads the meaning which applies to the following day— special importance attaches to the suit colours which will certainly show whether that day will be a fortunate one or not.

In many cases the inner meaning of the cards is never considered at all, this method being used on the Continent to determine, simply and solely, which will be the fortunate and unfortunate days in the week—Sunday counting as the first day, of course. Remember that the right-hand card is the more important—for instance, a spade on the right and a club on the left would indicate that things would certainly go wrong in the early part of the day, but would rapidly improve after noon. Whereas a club on the right and a spade on the left would indicate a prosperous morning, followed by a calamitous afternoon and evening.

When using this simple form of divination, no list of meanings has to be consulted. It is therefore an excellent companion method to the one already described for answering questions by the suit colours of the cards turned up.

Fourteen cards are turned up in this way, two and two, leaving the centre card face downwards on the table. The diviner should now note, on a slip of paper, the point values of each pair of cards, in case the enquirer should be confronted on that day by any business or other matter in which figures are concerned, For instance, if a nine of spades and a seven of hearts are the cards for the following Tuesday (the third day), then anything involving nine or any multiple of nine should be avoided, and those things involving seven should be followed up. Suppose someone calls and wishes to make an appointment, fix the seventh, fourteenth, twenty-first, or twenty-eighth day of the month. Should the *seventh day* (*i.e.*, the next Tuesday) fall on the ninth, eighteenth, or twenty-seventh of the month, it would obviously be a bad day to select. In the same way, if the fourteenth, twenty-first, or twenty-eighth of the month was the ninth day following, that also would prove a bad day.

With all these particulars to help him or her along, your client should be able to avoid all mishaps and make the best use of the opportunities for good fortune that might come his or her way.

The fifteenth card is used to answer one question, which, in this case, must be a spoken one. The suit of the card determines whether the answer is to be 'yes'; 'probably'; 'doubtful'; or 'no'—and the pip value should be noted if it can be made to fit in any way, as that particular number will have a fateful influence, one way or another, over the matter in question. Its influence, however, only lasts for the week in question, so if it is a spade, it is wise to warn your client to delay and wait for a more propitious time before proceeding with the matter in mind.

The interpretations given to the suits are:

Clubs   — Yes
Hearts   — Probably
Diamonds — Doubtful
Spades   — No

THREE QUESTIONS ANSWERED

This is a simple method of divination that does not require any consultation of tables of meanings. The pack of thirty-two cards must be well shuffled by the enquirer and cut into three unequal heaps, using the left hand. That portion of the pack that was previously on the top is now placed at the bottom; the middle section is placed above this; and the original bottom section is placed on top.

The cards are now spread out fanwise on the table, face downwards, taking care that every card is visible and that none overlap and hide a neighbouring card. The enquirer must now think of a question, and while doing so should choose three cards and place them, face downwards, on the table.

He or she should now think of the second question, and while doing so pick out seven cards, placing them separately on the table, also face downwards. While the third question is being thought of, thirteen cards must be chosen and the remainder of the pack discarded.

The diviner now turns up the first heap of three cards and determines from these the answer to the question—in this method the lower the value of the cards the less the opposition to the success of the enquirer, the more fortunate the result of the enquiry. The suit colours must also be considered as affecting the result, but the greater importance rests on the value of the cards—in this case the Ace is counted as the lowest and most fortunate card in the pack.

Similarly the second heap of seven cards, and the third heap of thirteen will be turned up, each in its turn, and the answer considered.

This is not only a simple but a quick method of divination, but obviously it only applies to answers to definite questions.

DIVINATION BY OBSTACLES

Have a pack of thirty-two cards well shuffled and cut once only. Pick out the type card representing the enquirer and hold the rest of the pack face downwards in your hand. The type card is placed in the centre of the table, the top card from the pack is turned over and placed above the type card, the second card being similarly placed below. The third is now placed on the left and the fourth card on the right. The fifth card is placed upon the type card, covering it. The diviner now discards eight cards altogether, and, that being done, adds another card to each of the five in the same order as before—above, below, left, right, and upon the type card.

Discard eight more cards and place the final five cards as before, one by one, upon the heaps. Read each heap in turn, beginning with the one from above the type card, and only looking out for pairs and triplets, suit colour, and whether the four high cards (the Ace here being counted with the Court cards, as this method is older than the last one described) or the four low cards predominate—the latter being the personal effort of the enquirer, and the Court cards being the help or interference of other people.

DIVINATION BY PAIRS AND TRIPLETS

This method is not so old as some of the others but is very effective, besides being reliable.

The pack of thirty-two cards must be well shuffled and cut into three with the left hand, these being arranged as before explained, taking the original centre section for the bottom of the newly arranged pack. The prepared cards are now held in the left hand and the three top cards are turned up. If they contain two or three cards of the same face-value or three cards of the same suit, they should be placed face upwards on the table—the others being discarded.

This is repeated till the pack is exhausted, the odd two cards being discarded.

The discarded heap is now well shuffled and cut three times as before—this must always be done by the enquirer and never by the diviner, who merely deals or arranges the cards and gives their meanings as they appeal to him.

Diviners who are slightly clairvoyant make some marvellously accurate predictions without apparently studying the accepted meaning of the cards.

The cards having been shuffled the second time, leaving the selected pairs and triplets face upwards on the table, are again gone through in sets of three as before in order to increase the row of fateful cards on the table, any odd cards at the end being discarded as at first.

This process is repeated for a third time before the final fateful row of cards is consulted. You can now give a general opinion upon the prospects before the enquirer by a study of the prevailing suits and by noting whether Court cards or plain cards predominate, or you can go further and pick up the cards, two at a time, taking one from each end as in previous methods. This can always be done when cards are arranged in a row, by whatever process they have been selected— always bearing in mind that the right-hand card is more active and positive than the left-hand one.

A quick, though perhaps rough and ready, method of divination is to let the enquirer choose thirteen cards at random after the pack has been well shuffled and cut once. As chosen, they are placed face upwards across the table from left to right, and the answer to the question is decided by the predominant suits and by the number of Court or plain cards thus selected. Should there be an equal number of cards belonging to two or more suits (obviously with thirteen cards there cannot be an equal number of Court or plain cards), you give preference to that suit that has most cards on the right of the row—these being more active and aggressive.

DIVINATION BY THE SPADE SUIT

The pack must be shuffled and cut into three heaps and rebuilt, as before explained.

The diviner now holds the pack face upwards—this is different from most methods of divination, where the cards are generally dealt from the top of the pack. Each card is looked at, but unless it is a spade, it is placed on the table, face upwards, to form a fresh pack. As soon as a spade is reached, that card is also discarded, but the next following card is placed, face upwards, on the table to start the necessary fateful row of cards. Should two or more spades come together, only the first one is discarded, the other or others being added to the fateful row in front of you, together with the next card following the last of that batch of spades.

This is continued till the pack is exhausted, when the discarded heap is taken up and treated in the same fashion *without being re-shuffled*.

This process is repeated for a third time and then the type card must be looked for—if it is not already in the row, it must be found and added at the end. The diviner now counts the third, seventh, and thirteenth card from the type card, in each case counting the type card as one. These three cards are not removed from the row, but can be pulled down a little below the level of the others, as they form the dominant trio in this method.

This counting is done to the left, and when you reach the extreme card, the one first put on the table, you go back to the end card at the right and so continue your count if necessary. But it often happens that all three dominant cards are reached before you come to the card on the extreme left. Of these three cards, the one finally nearest the right is the most powerful. It clearly depends upon the position in the row of the type card itself whether the third, seventh, or thirteenth is the important card.

It is generally agreed that by this method only near events can be predicted, certainly it does not cover more than a month.

A somewhat similar method is used with the full pack, but instead of using the spade suit as the guide for the cards to be picked out, you go by the points of the cards—the Ace in this method counts as one. The pack having been shuffled and cut into three heaps and rebuilt as before, you deal the cards from the top, placing each one face upwards on the table as you do so. While you do this, you count aloud: one, two, three, four, five, six, seven, eight, nine, ten, Jack, Queen, King, one, etc.

If any card, irrespective of suit, turns up at the proper count—for instance, if the fifth card really is a five, it is placed as one of the fateful row, and the counting continues as before.

When the pack is exhausted, the discarded cards are turned over and dealt out again as before, turning each one up in the spade suit method; but you must be careful after the second time to note at which card you cease calling, as when you start the third deal you do not restart the counting at one, but continue from where you left off.

In addition to the cards that turn up at their own proper calls, you also add to the fateful row any cards that turn up three or more at a time, whether at their proper call or not. Thus three tens, three fives, would be added, merely because they follow each other in value, but three hearts or three spades would be ignored, as in this method the dealing takes no account of suits.

The diviner now forms a rough cross from the cards in the row, placing the first card from the extreme left to form the top of the cross; the next card to form the bottom of the cross; the third to form the right, and the fourth the left. The next four cards are built above these in the same way—top, bottom, right, left, and so you build the cross until all the chosen cards are used up.

The top heap is read first, as the predictions from those cards are supposed to come first; then the bottom heap; then the right and then the left—the latter, of course, being very far into the future. You can allow roughly a fortnight for each heap.

THE DECISION BY ACES

The pack of thirty-two cards must be well shuffled and cut into three and rebuilt. The diviner now turns up three cards at a time—if an Ace appears among them, or the type card representing the enquirer, or the Wish card (nine of hearts), those three cards must be taken out and placed face upwards on the table. This continues until the six cards are all exposed, i.e., the four Aces, type card, and the Wish card. Those sets of three cards not containing one or more of the six fateful cards are to be discarded altogether.

When the necessary cards are obtained, they must be gathered together, re-shuffled and cut, and dealt out once more in sets of three, retaining those sets only that contain one or more of the six cards of Fate. This is repeated for a third time—if the six cards are now gathered together within a total of nine cards (or fewer) the Wish will prove successful. If in twelve, the result is doubtful; but if over twelve, the reply is negative. If under nine, then the fewer the cards, the quicker and more decisive the result.

The following is the record of an actual test and will show how it works: The type card was the King of clubs, as a dark man was the enquirer. The first three cards turned up were the King of diamonds, Ace of spades, and King of clubs—these were retained on the table, as they included both an Ace and the type card. The second set were the King of spades, Queen of spades, and ten of diamonds—these were discarded as useless. The third set were the ten of hearts, the six of diamonds, and the King of Hearts, and were also discarded. The fourth set were the seven of spades, the eight of spades, and the Ace of diamonds, and were kept. The fifth set contained the nine of diamonds, eight of clubs, and Ace of clubs, and of course were retained. The sixth set were the Jack of clubs, ten of spades, and Ace of hearts, and were left on the table; while the seventh set completed the first deal, as it contained the Jack of spades, nine of hearts, and five of clubs.

The remainder of the pack, therefore, was added to the discarded heap, and the fifteen cards, face upwards, on the table, were gathered together, well shuffled, and again dealt in sets of three, with the following result: first came the Ace of spades, nine of hearts, and Jack of spades; then the ten of spades, Ace of hearts, and nine of diamonds. These were followed by the King of diamonds, five of clubs, and Jack of clubs, and of course, these three cards were at once discarded to the satisfaction of the enquirer. Then came a set consisting of the seven of spades, Ace of diamonds, and eight of clubs, which were retained; and, finally, the eight of spades, Ace of clubs, and the King of clubs, which were also kept.

These twelve cards were now gathered and shuffled for the third and fateful deal, the result of which was as follows: the first set contained the Ace of hearts, nine of hearts, and the King of clubs—a very good start, giving us three of the necessary cards at once. The second set contained the nine of diamonds, Jack of spades, and eight of clubs, indicating some obstacle or difficulty to be faced, as none of these cards were of any use and clearly delayed the gratification of the enquirer's wish. Then came the Ace of clubs, Ace of spades, and ten of spades, thus destroying all hope of immediate success —but the final set commenced with the Ace of diamonds, thus enabling us to get out at the tenth card. This is quite good, and shows success after some small delay or difficulty— indeed, it is always reckoned satisfactory if the six fateful cards can be secured at the eleventh. Six or seven would show startling and unexpected good fortune; eight or nine is extremely fortunate; ten or eleven quite satisfactory; twelve or thirteen are very doubtful; while fourteen or fifteen may be looked upon as a distinct negative.

There is another way of deciding a question by the Aces which is a general favourite and is considered reliable.

The pack, being well shuffled, is cut once only with the left hand. Thirteen cards are then dealt from the top, face upwards, and if any Aces are among them, they (the Aces only) are retained. The pack is now reshuffled and cut, and again thirteen cards are dealt and any Aces are removed. This is repeated a third time and if, in these three deals, the four Aces have all been secured, the enquirer may feel satisfied that a wish will be granted.

Should the Aces be secured in the second deal, or in the first (a very rare occurrence), the result naturally will be much more favourable. But if in the three deals only three Aces are secured, the result is doubtful—whereas if fewer than three turn up, the wish will not be gratified.

There is still another method of working by the Aces—it is rather more elaborate and a favourable result is not so easily obtained. First of all pick out the four Aces, the type card to represent the enquirer, the nine of spades to represent disappointment, and a seventh card to represent the question itself—if about money, this would be the ten of diamonds; if about business, then the ten of clubs; if about a woman, then the Queen nearest to her in suit colour; if about a man, then the corresponding King. For any general wish, choose the Jack of the enquirer's own suit to represent the enquirer's thoughts.

These seven cards are shuffled but not cut, and are then spread, face downwards, in a row on the table. The remainder of the cards are then shuffled well and cut once and are turned up in a row on the table, seven at a time. The object is to find the Wish card, represented by the nine of hearts. Should this card appear in the row of seven, count its position from the left and turn over the corresponding card in the row of fateful cards lying, face downwards, on the table. Should the nine of hearts not appear in the first seven cards repeat the process as before until you come to it.

If the card thus reversed is the nine of spades, that settles the enquiry at once by an emphatic negative—if not, the whole performance is repeated and a second card reversed in the fateful row of seven. If the fateful nine of spades is once more avoided, the process is repeated for a third time—the appearance of the Disappointment card after the second deal is not, of course, so emphatic as if it is reversed at once, but it is still a negative, though with no attendant disaster or unpleasantness. If it is discovered after the third deal, there is still a chance of success if the enquirer is keen enough to take the necessary trouble over the matter.

The methods given so far are all well-known and in universal use, but in the present chapter some very effective methods of telling have been given, which at the same time are perfectly simple. Four of these methods can be used at once by the student, as no list of meanings has to be learnt or studied—these four methods are 'The Four Aces'; 'A Week's Happenings'; 'Three Questions Answered'; and 'Decision by Aces'.

5

♥ ♣ ♦ ♠

DOMINOES AND DICE

It is claimed by some of the ancient writers that dominoes were first made for fortune-telling purposes and that the games now played with them were an afterthought. Whether this is true or not, we cannot say; but it is certainly a fact that dominoes have long been used to determine what the Fates have planned for our future.

When seeking to gain the prophecy of the dominoes, you must act in the following manner if an accurate reading is to be secured.

First, let the dominoes be placed, face down, on the table. The person concerned then sits at the table with his or her back to the fire or fireplace. Next, the dominoes are swirled round and round until the person can honestly say that location of any particular one of them is not known. That done, the enquirer places the left hand over as many of the dominoes as it will conveniently cover and the enquirer revolves it through a complete circle, taking an anti-clockwise direction. A last requirement is that the person must declare aloud that he or she has not sought a horoscope from the dominoes since the last new moon, then, with the left hand, picks out any one of the dominoes he or she chooses. Its message is as follows:

Double six—Things are favourable to you. Love and finance will prosper.

Six-five—You are due to rise up in the world, but not without a certain amount of antagonism from those who pose as your friends.

Six-four—There is prosperity ahead for you, if you act sensibly. Note, however, that people with whom you are well acquainted will endeavour to rob you of your deserts.

Six-three—Make up your mind to be determined over the things that are dear to your heart. Do this and you will have cause to rejoice.

Six-two—Many good things are waiting for you to take them, but there is much fear that you may let them slip from out of your grasp.

Six-one—It is very plainly indicated that you will never experience your full share of troubles.

Six-blank—Your love affairs will give you far more happiness than the reverse.

Double five—Be prepared for changes. You have the power to use them for good or for ill.

Five-four—Money is not going to be a source of comfort for you. It will give rise to difficulties.

Five-three—You will make money by hard work and every penny you acquire will have to be earned.

Five-two—Married life for you is or will be a thing of joy and comfort, as long as you do what is right.

Five-one—There is happiness awaiting you. It will be derived either from family ties or from riches, but not from both.

Five-blank—You are likely to burn your fingers while playing with love.

Double four—You have an abundance of determination which will take you a long way.

Four-three—Your financial conditions are about to undergo a change.

Four-two—You have a roving instinct and there are signs that travelling is likely to bring you a certain measure of success or happiness.

Four-one—You do not do yourself justice. There are many roads to success which you could take; but you miss them all.

Four-blank—Look at 'Five-blank' and take the hint very much to heart.

Double three—Life is prepared to offer you a great deal. Do not throw away your chances.

Three-two—Rise above the petty worries of life and your love affairs should prosper.

Three-one—Business matters are likely to cause you apprehension, but there is no reason why you should not smile even at them.

Three-blank—Approach love in the spirit it deserves and you will have few causes for worry.

Double two—You are the kind of person who will derive the highest joys from marriage and the possession of a family.

Two-one—For you there is a special significance in the saying, 'Marry in haste and repent at leisure.'

Two-blank—You are likely to experience a tangle of marriage and money. Go cautiously when these are concerned.

Double one—There is no reason to suppose that you will ever rise to fame. Nevertheless, you will be happy enough in your own sphere.

One-blank—You are to experience a piece of luck very soon. It will come in an unexpected manner.

Double blank—Life for you will continue to be uneventful.

THE DICE DECIDE

Take two dice, shake them up in a cup and throw them out on to a table. Then note the spots which are showing.

If you have previously written a reasonable wish on a slip of paper here is what the dice say about this wish:

Double six—Undoubtedly, it will come true.

Six-five—Most likely it will be granted.

Six-four—Yes, it will come true.

Six-three—It is hardly likely to happen.

Six-two—There are signs that it will not be granted.

Six-one—It will be granted.

Double five—There is no doubt whatever. It will happen.

Five-four—No, it cannot come true.

Five-three—There is not much chance that it will be granted.

Five-two—Perhaps it will be granted.

Five-one—It is fifty-fifty.

Double four—It might and it might not happen.

Four-three—Yes, it will happen for sure.

Four-two—It is not very likely to happen.

Four-one—There is more chance that it will, than it will not, happen.

Double three—If you act reasonably, it is sure to come true.

Three-two—It is almost bound to be granted.

Three-one—There is not much hope of it happening.

Double two—Not the slightest chance of it coming to pass.

Two-one—It will be granted.

Double one—The Fates refuse to say anything about the matter. They remain silent.

It should be remembered that the dice cup ought to be shaken and emptied by using the left hand, and it is always advisable to shake the dice so that they revolve in the cup with an anticlockwise motion.